CREATURES WITH COCKS

CREATURES WITH COCKS

First published in 2006

Summersdale Publishers Ltd
46 West Street
Chichester
West Sussex
PO19 1RP
UK

www.summersdale.com

Printed and bound in Poland

ISBN: 978-1-84953-933-3

Substantial discounts on bulk quantities of Summersdale books are available to corporations, professional associations and other organisations. For details contact Nicky Douglas by telephone: +44 (0) 1243 756902, fax: +44 (0) 1243 786300 or email: nicky@summersdale.com.

CREATURES WITH COCKS

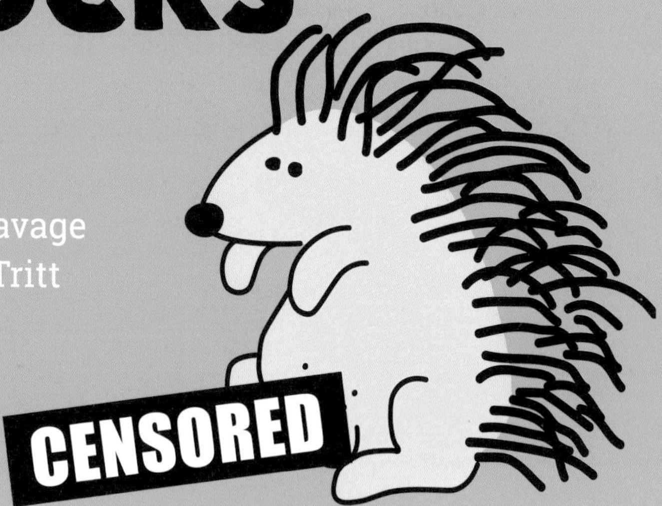
CENSORED

Monty Savage
& Oscar Tritt

summersdale

Contents

Chapter 1
Creatures of the Land

Hissing Cockroach

Loves utter filth – the dirtier the better.

HISS

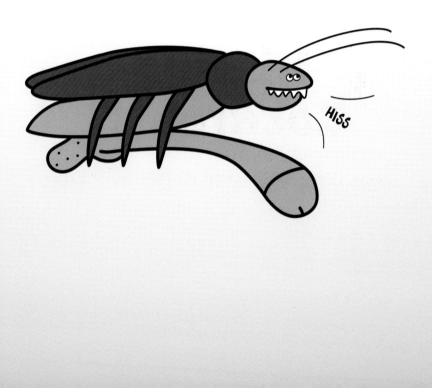

Pork-upine

Able to mate from a safe distance.

Kangaroo

Can make single bounds of up to 30 feet,
over non-prickly ground.

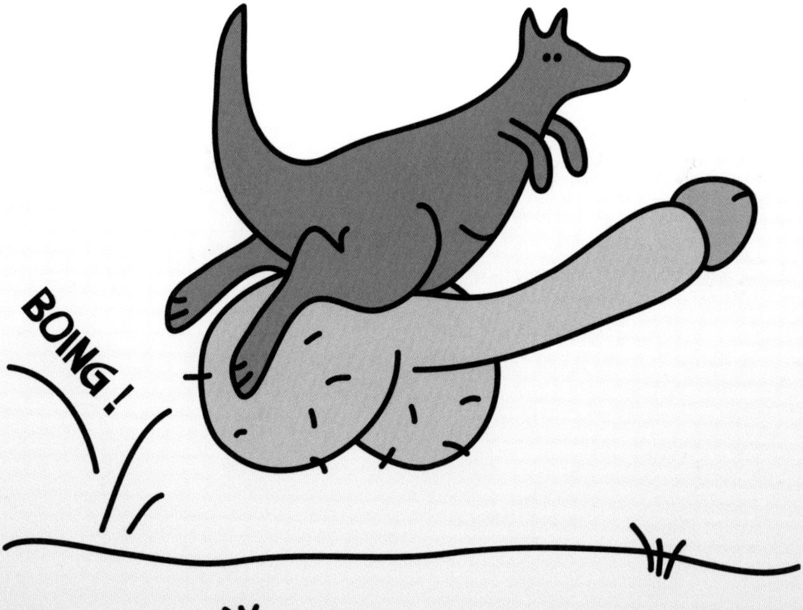
BOING!

Mombasan
Shaft Mouse

Extinct, due to inability to move or hunt.

The Black Memba

Long, fast and very dangerous if it gets in your pants.

Armadildo

Hunted to extinction by fierce, buxom
Amazons who had a strange passion
for its meat.

Stick Insect

Struggles to fool predators into thinking it's only a twig and two berries.

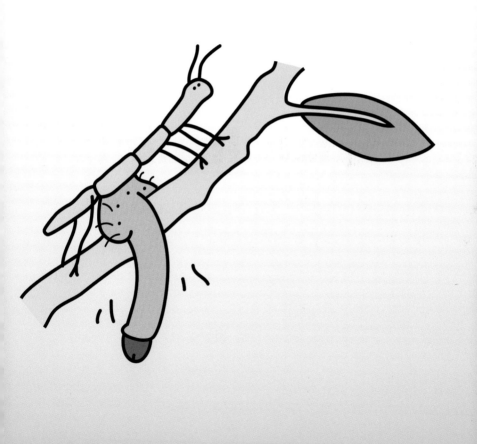

Cocktus

Technically not a creature, but still
a wonder of nature.

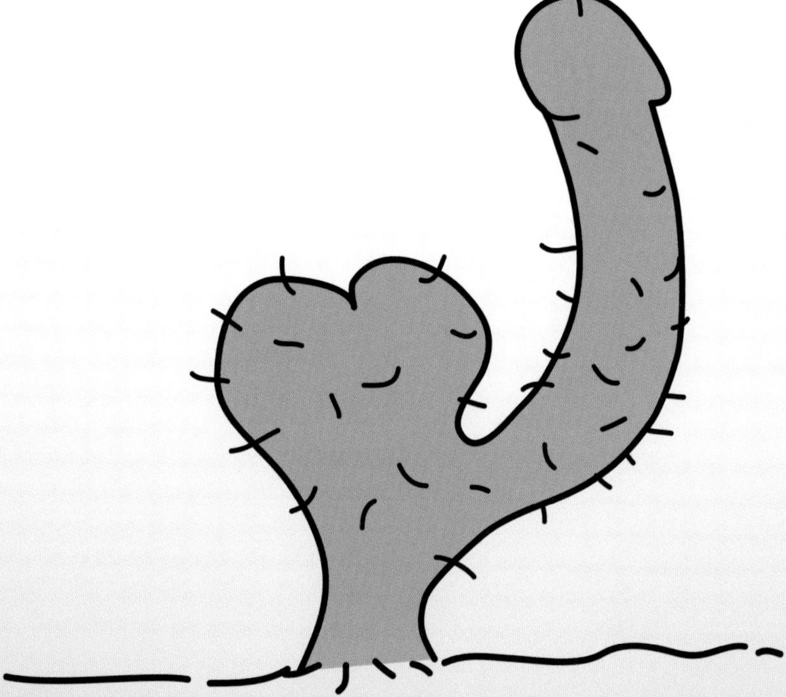

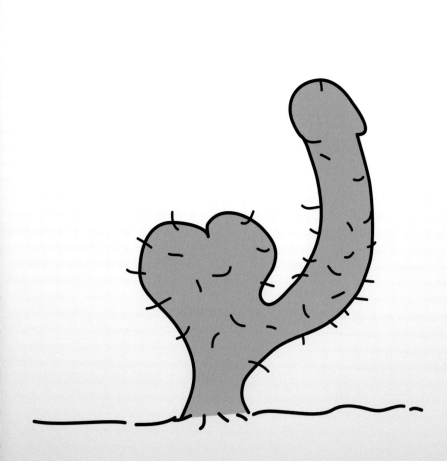

Almost-hidden Tree Sloth

Prefers tall trees.

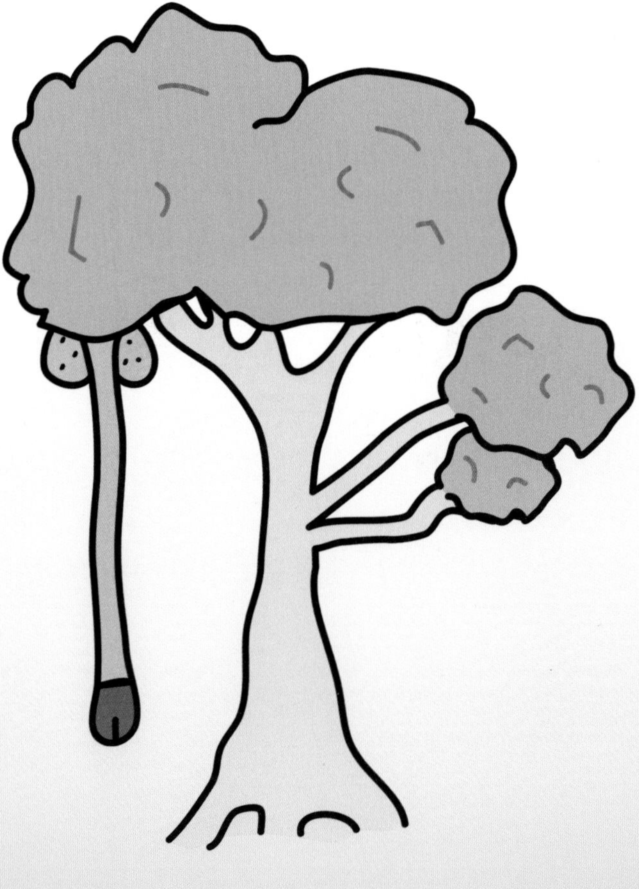

Rhin-oh

The Rhin-oh's horn is fabled as a
monstrous aphrodisiac.

Chapter 2

Creatures of the Air

Common
Teste Fly

A swarm of these summer pests
can drive campers nuts.

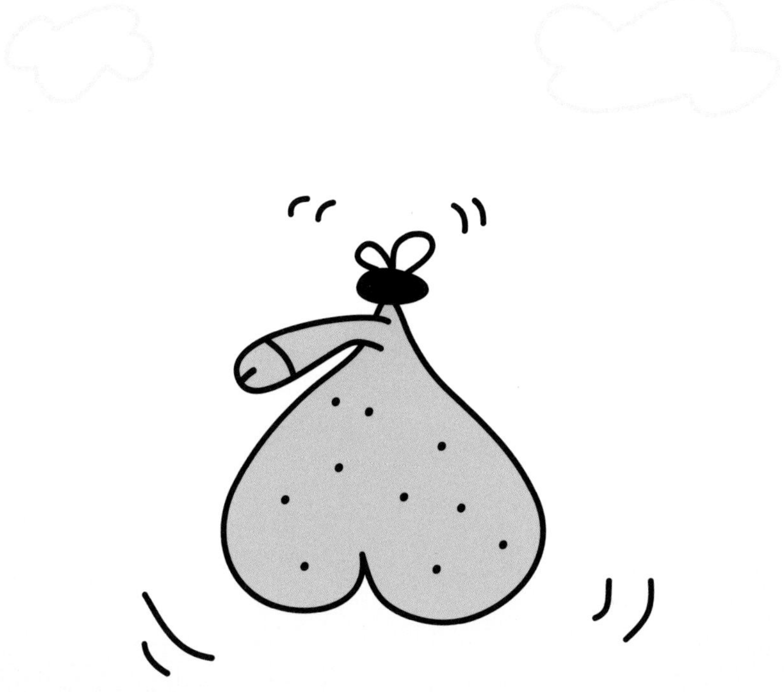

Cock Robin

The male is a proud, devoted parent.

Pterodicktyl

Due to the trauma and discomfort of landing, this ancient creature would sometimes stay aloft for days.

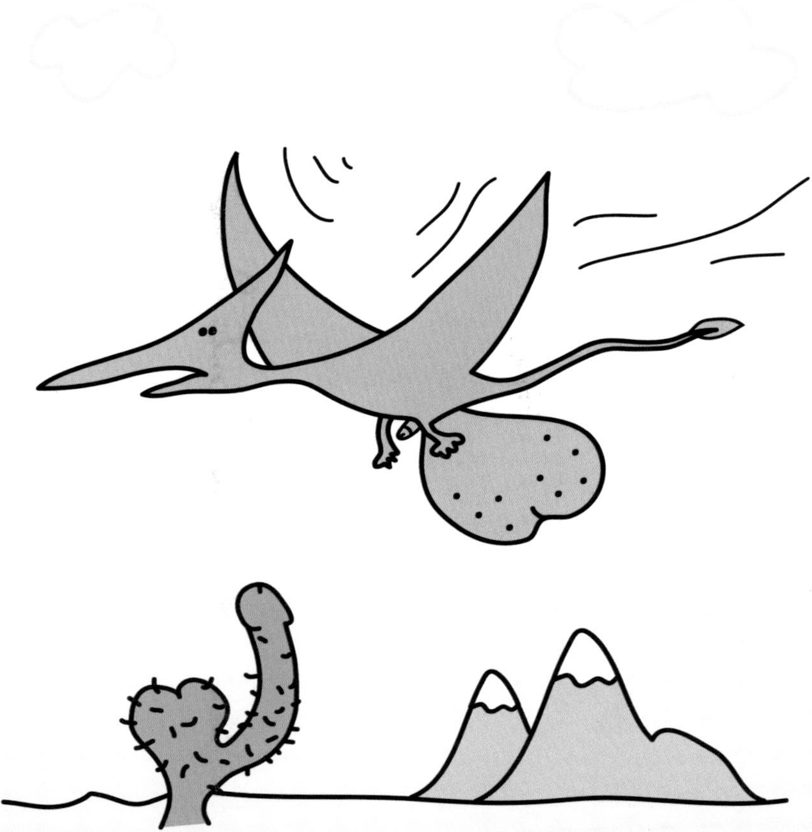

Bat

Well hung.

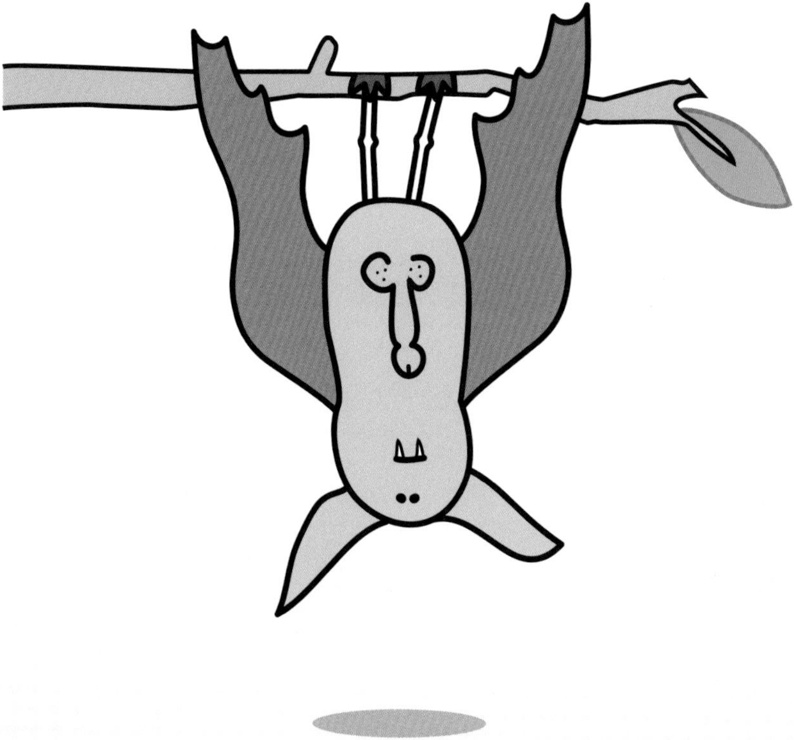

Cockatwo

Often faints when excited.

Flying Squirrel

Thrives on a diet of nuts.

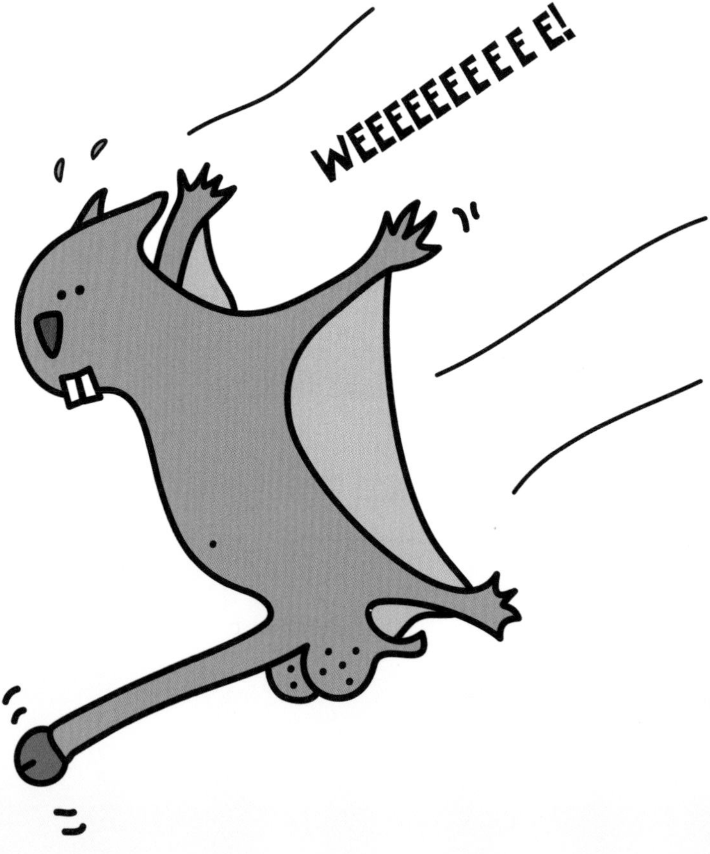
WEEEEEEEEE E!

Owl

Stays up all night.

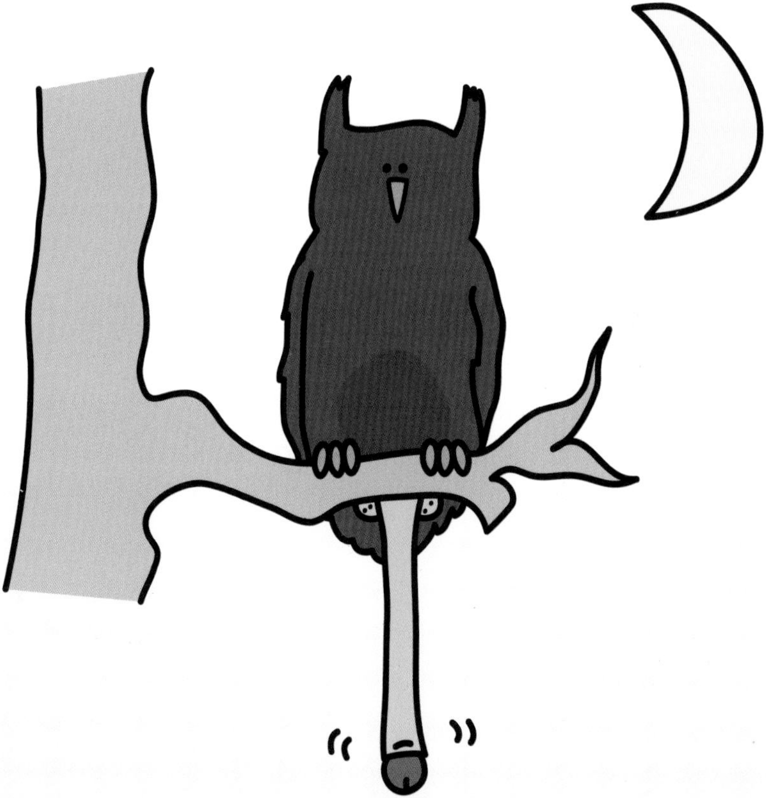

Wood-pecker

Believed extinct because the male couldn't
tell the wood from the trees.

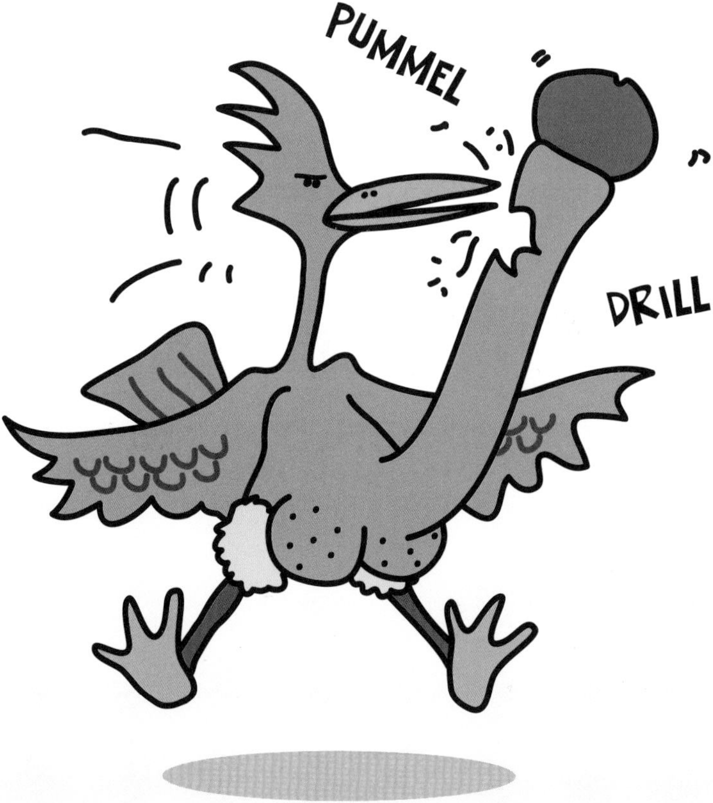
PUMMEL
DRILL

Ostrich

Finds it hard to get off the ground.

Chapter 3
Creatures of the Water

Cocktopus

When roused, this creature provides stiff
opposition to any predator.

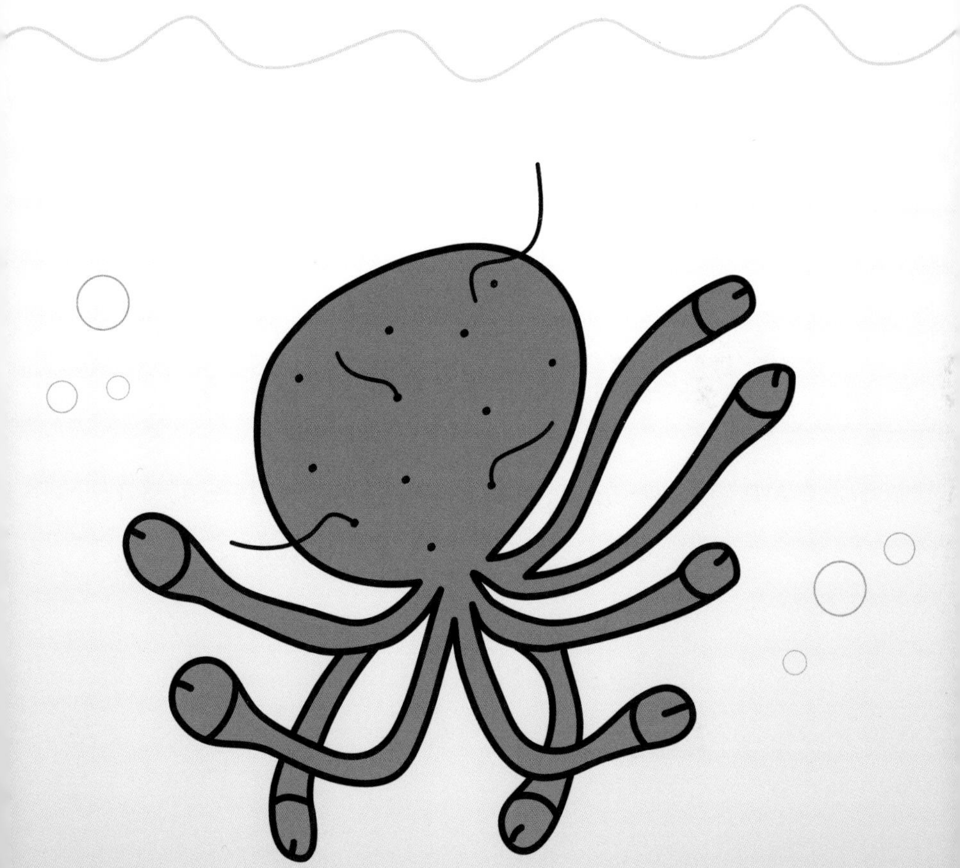

Dangler Fish

Evolution's first unsuccessful attempt at this unique hunting method.

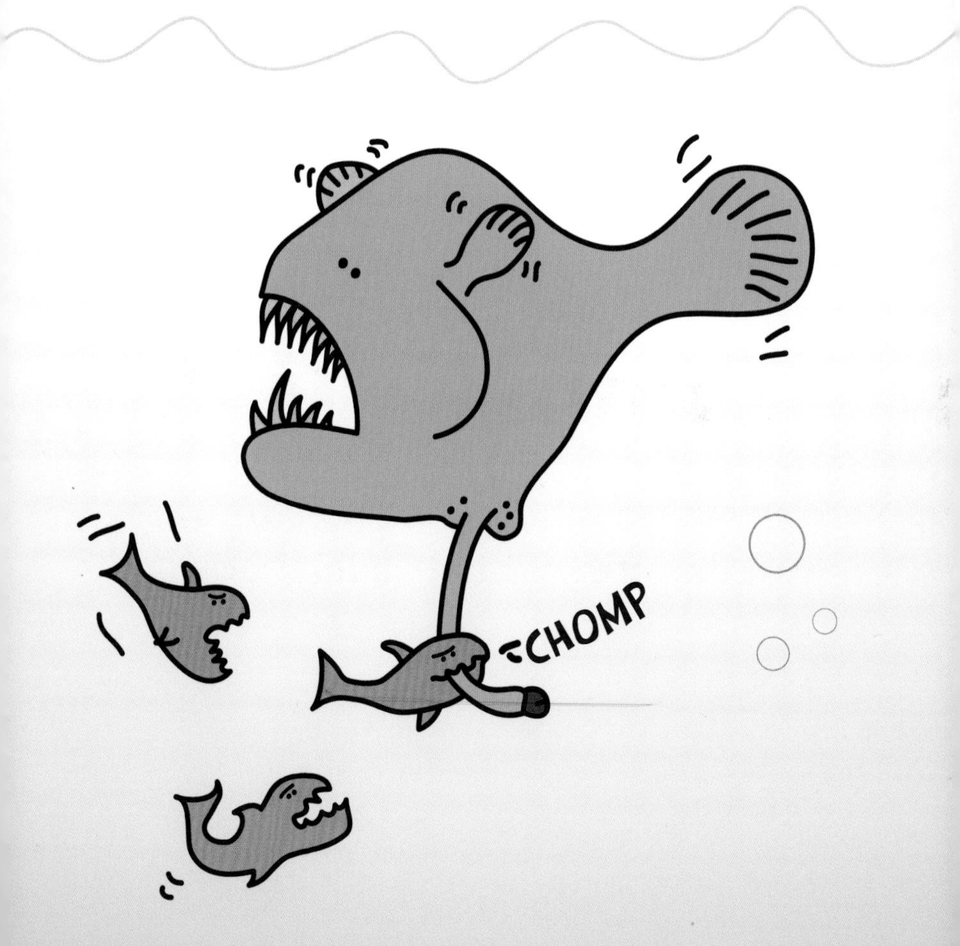
CHOMP

Smallrus

Can endure sub-zero temperatures, but with the side effect of some shrinkage.

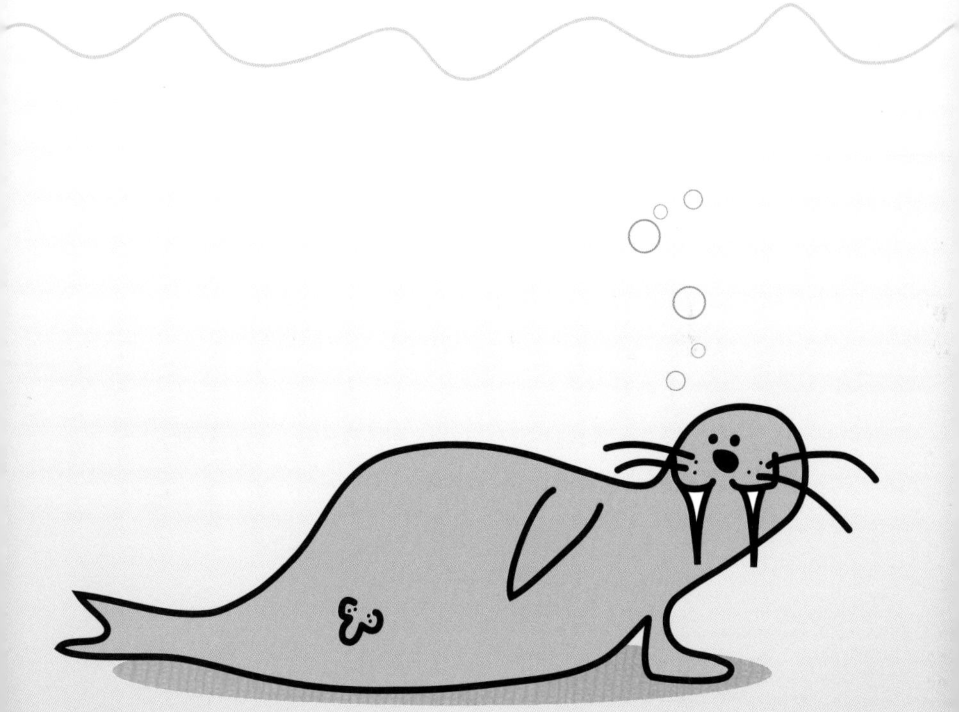

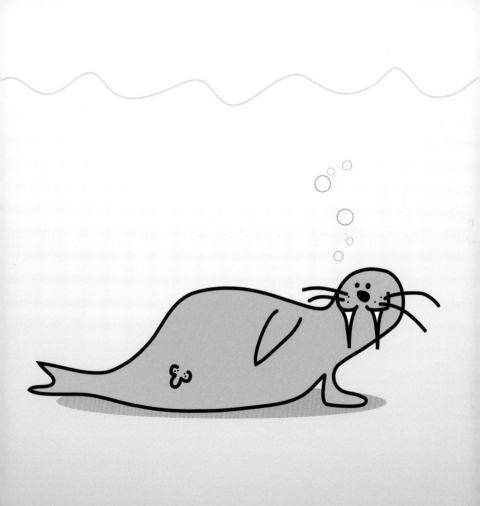

Platypuss

Leads a simple life exploring the
wilds down under.

Cockodile

Has just one natural predator.

Deep-sea Clam

A shy and retiring bottom feeder.

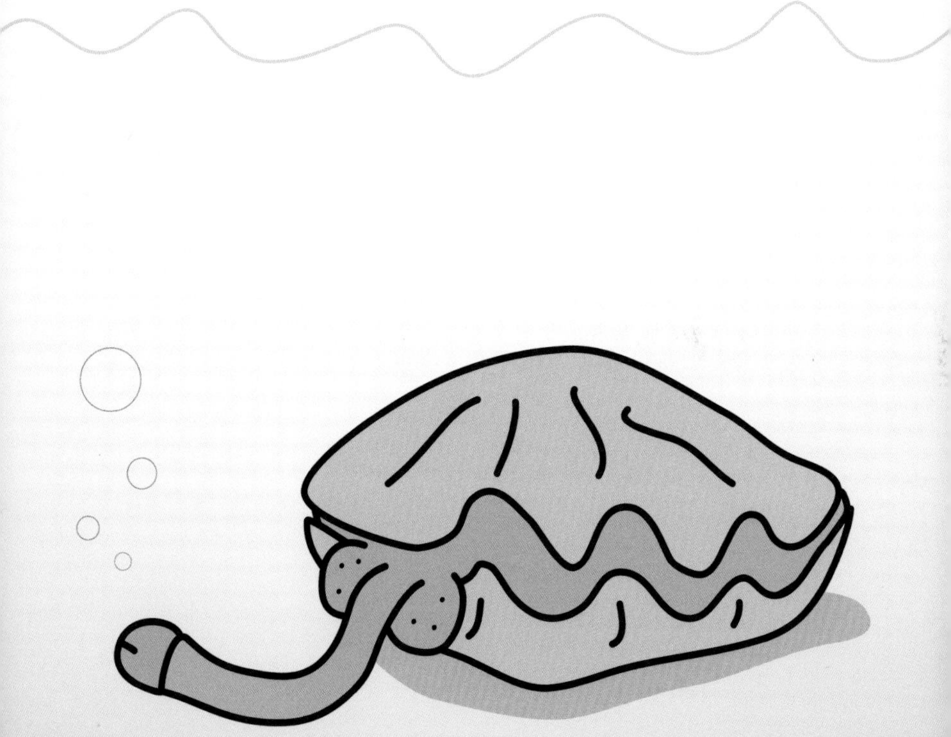

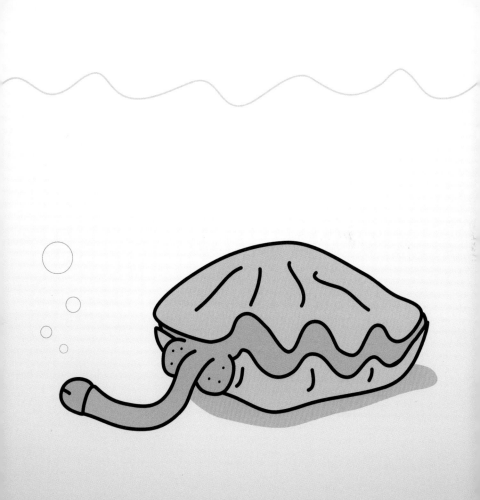

Pork-sword Fish

Evolution has thankfully blunted its tip.

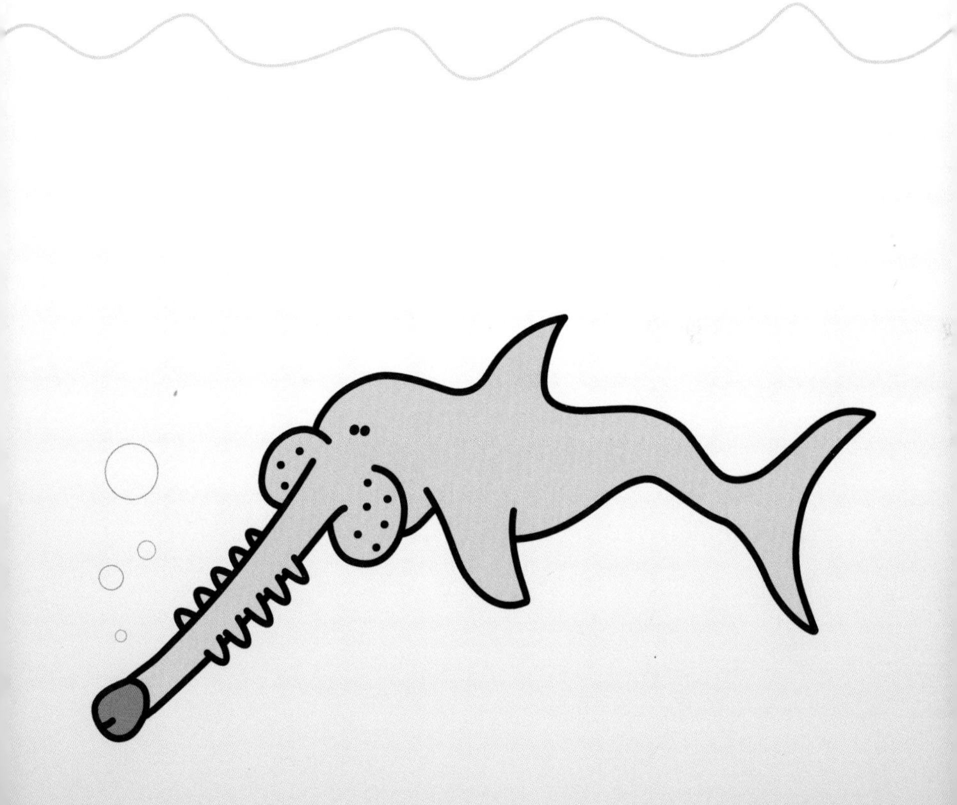

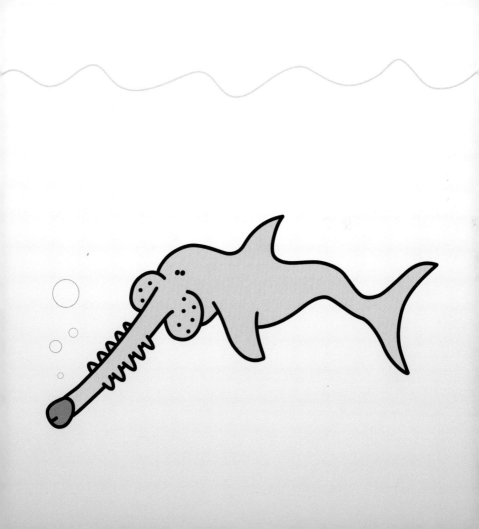

Trigger Fish

In times of stress, trigger fish deploy their only natural defence.

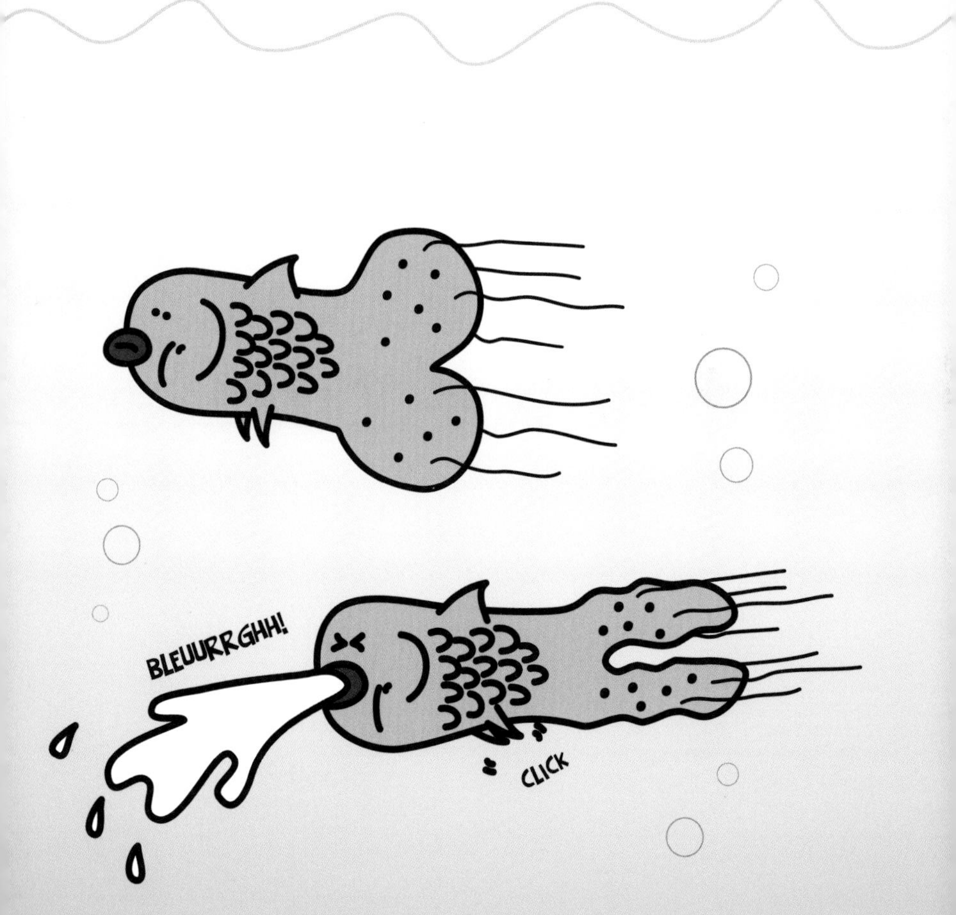
BLEUURRGHH!
CLICK

Oceanic Turtle

Commonly plagued by crabs.

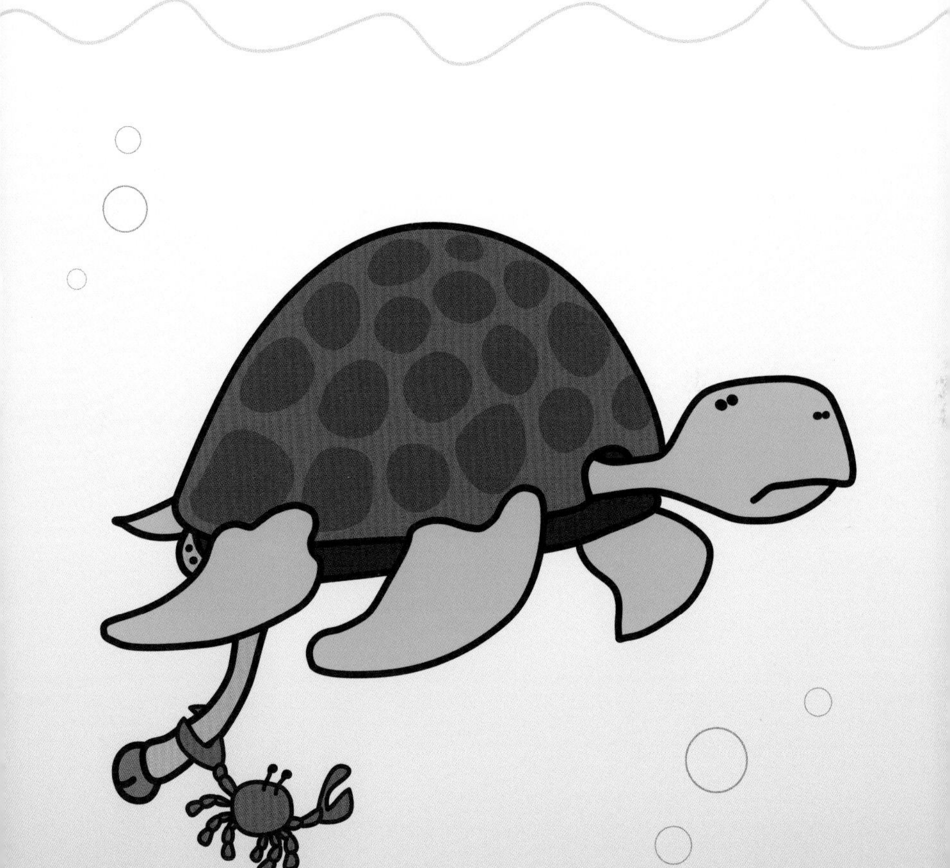

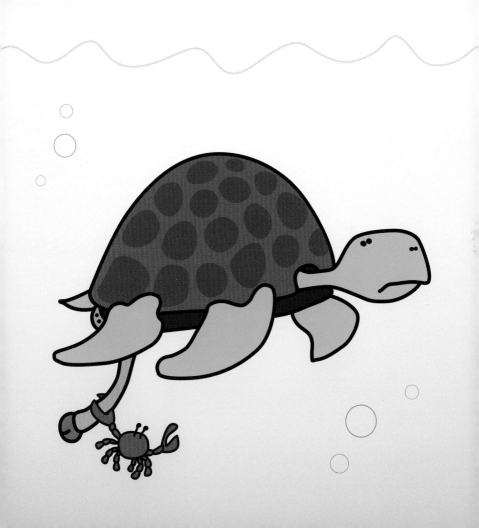

Penguin

In the depths of winter, the male
fishes with live bait.

Wankton

A crucial source of nourishment for other creatures who inhabit the seas.

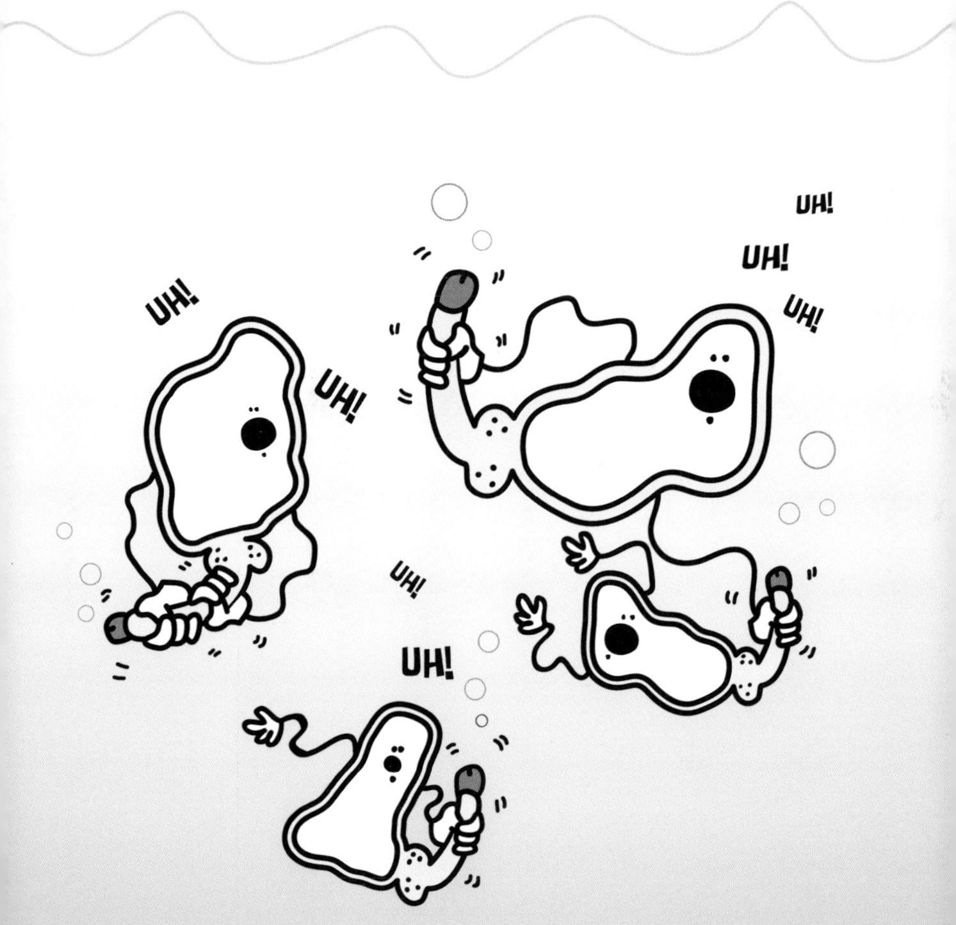
UH!
UH!
UH!
UH!
UH!
UH!
UH!
UH!

Chapter 4
Creatures of Legend

SHUFFLE

Mandusa

Just one glimpse of the hideous Mandusa
will instantly petrify your manhood.

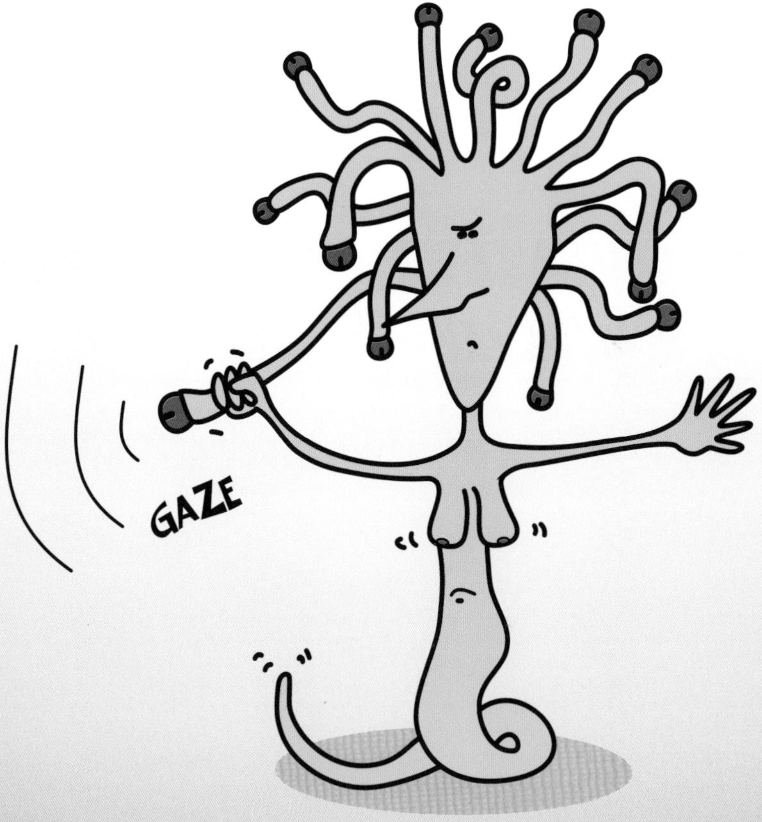
GAZE

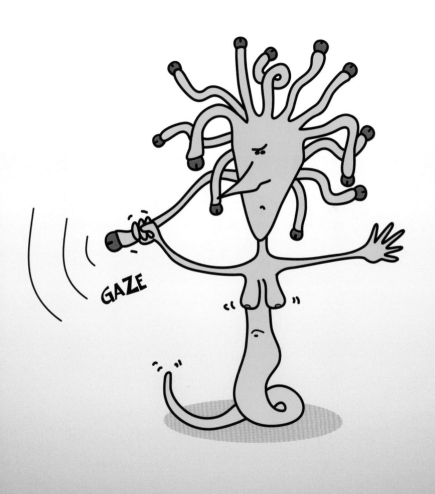

Nobferatu: The Shaft of Darkness

Cock of the Undead.

MINCE

Moby Dick

The scourge of the high seas.

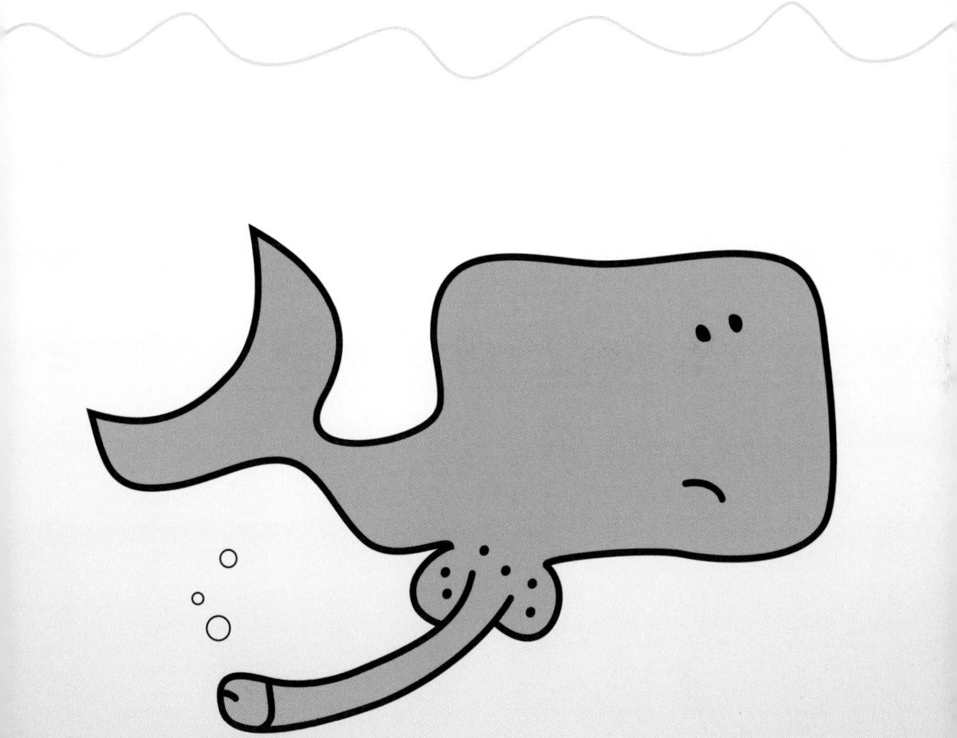

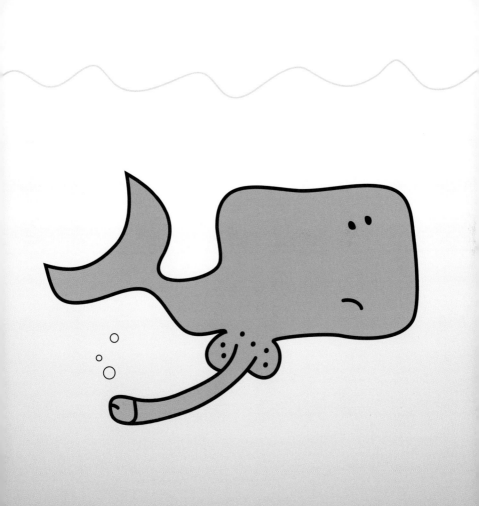

Cyclops

Not called 'Old One-eye' for the
reason you think.

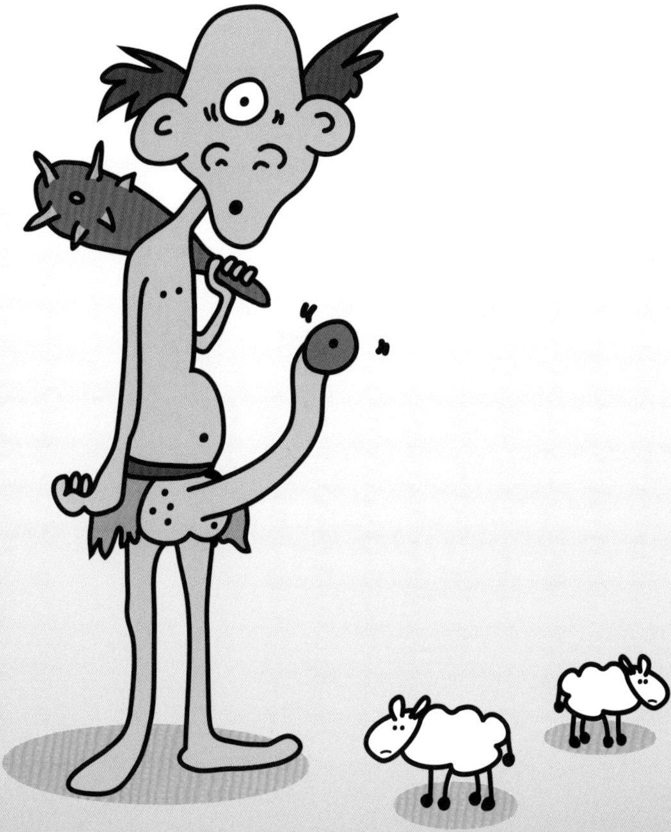

Cockenstein's Monster

An abomination made of human parts.

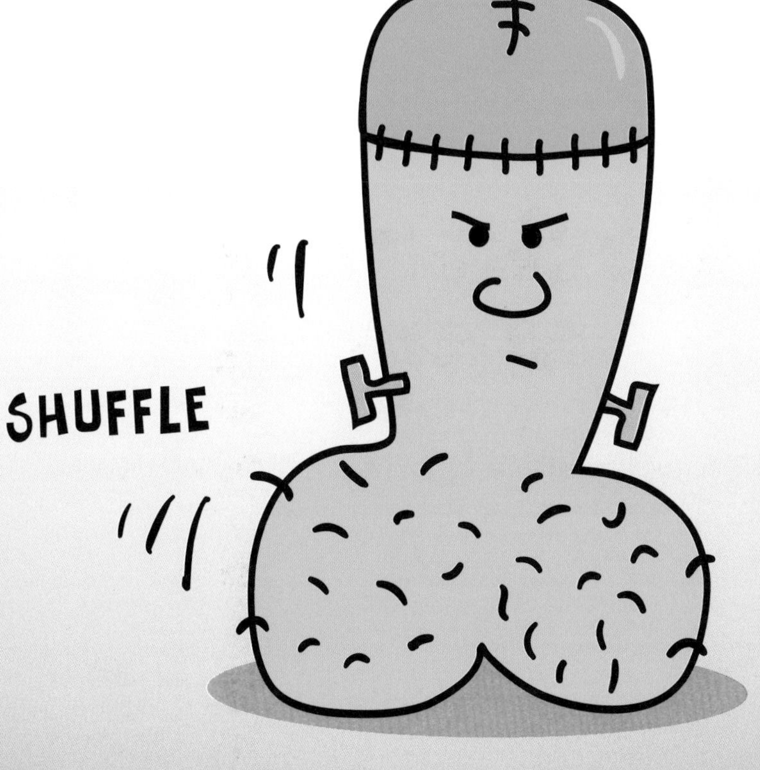
SHUFFLE

Bigfoot

To its eternal shame, its feet are the only
big thing about this creature.

King Kock

Forty feet of rippling, primal love muscle.

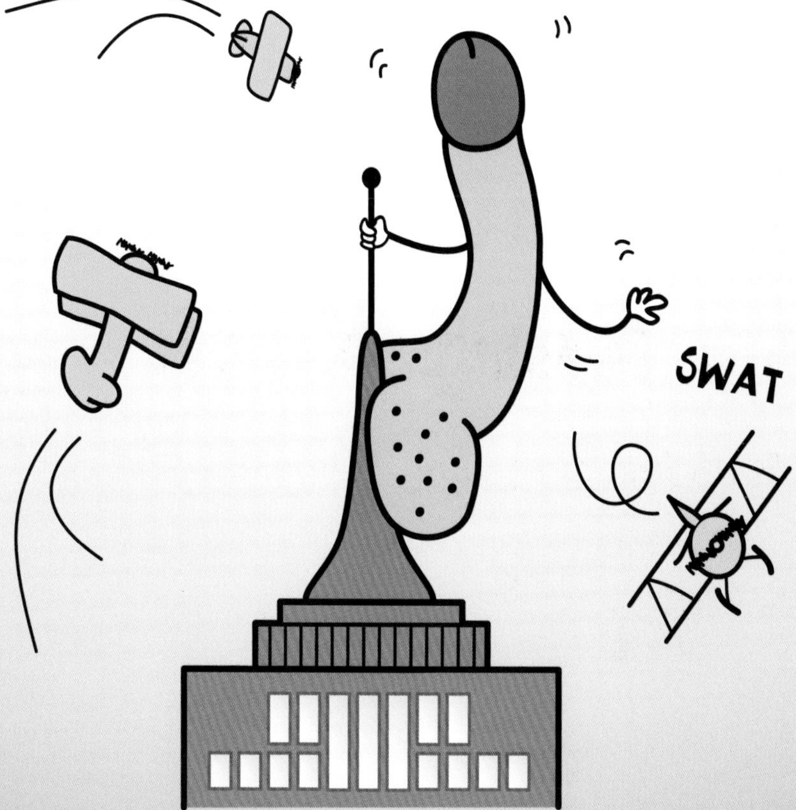
SWAT

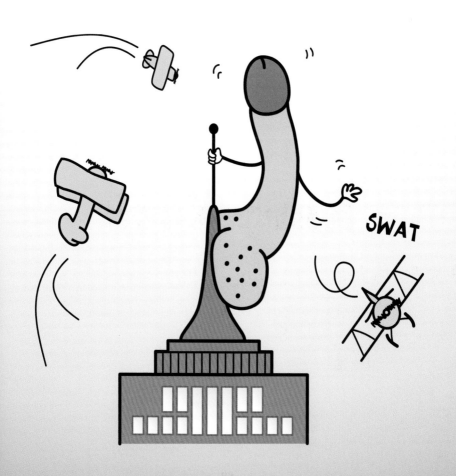

The Elusive Cock Ness Monster

Lurks in the dark nether regions of Scotland.

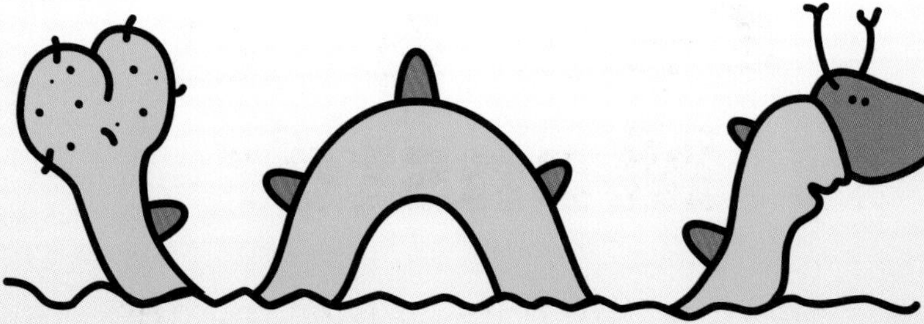

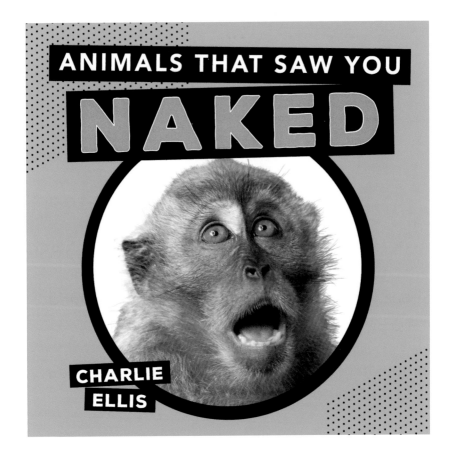

ANIMALS THAT SAW YOU

NAKED

CHARLIE ELLIS

ANIMALS THAT SAW YOU NAKED

Charlie Ellis

Hardback

978-1-84953-768-1

£6.99

Shock. Horror. Pain. Fear. These are the emotions every animal feels when they see a human naked. This book exposes the effects of our wanton behaviour and reveals the true feelings our furry (and feathered) friends can no longer hide.

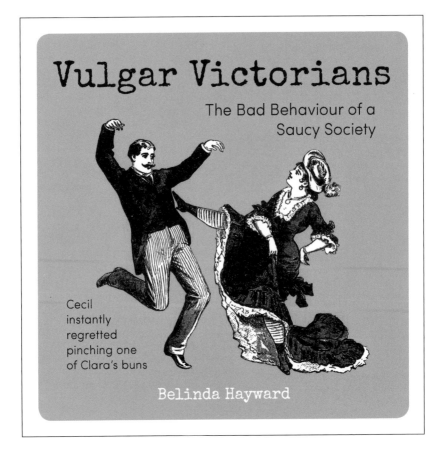

Vulgar Victorians

The Bad Behaviour of a
Saucy Society

Cecil
instantly
regretted
pinching one
of Clara's buns

Belinda Hayward

VULGAR VICTORIANS
The Bad Behaviour of a Saucy Society

Belinda Hayward

Hardback

978-1-84953-791-9

£7.99

See the past with new eyes as you dive into the no-holds-barred humour of *Vulgar Victorians*.

This showcase of rude prudes reveals a world that is both historical and hysterical.

If you're interested in finding out more about our books, find us on Facebook at **Summersdale Publishers** and follow us on Twitter at **@Summersdale**.

www.summersdale.com

www.creatureswithcocks.com